MEASURING INVESTMENT PERFORMANCE

IN ACCOUNTS WITH DEPOSITS OR WITHDRAWALS

Savings Account Building Up to Retirement
Retirement Account Providing Funds in Retirement

Return on Investment (ROI)
Dietz Modification of ROI
Time-Weighted Return (TWR)
Internal Rate of Return (IRR)
SEC Total Return

Harold Jacobson

AuthorHouse™ LLC
1663 Liberty Drive
Bloomington, IN 47403
www.authorhouse.com
Phone: 1-800-839-8640

First edition
Email: nesteggcd@verizon.net

Published by AuthorHouse 01/02/2014

ISBN: 978-1-4918-3023-9 (sc)
ISBN: 978-1-4918-3030-7 (e)

Library of Congress Control Number: 2013919491

authorHOUSE®

PREFACE

The author was an aerospace engineer for 38 years, taught algebra at Santa Barbara City College for eleven years and then retired. To fill his time subsequently, he began to manage his retirement account---depositing and withdrawing funds, identifying stocks to purchase and sell. To grade his management he researched methods to calculate rates of return and discovered a hidden story behind the methods. This booklet tells this story as an algebra teacher would teach it.

The simple formula for Return on Investment during a period---the one you probably know by heart---does not compute in the presence of cash flows (deposits or withdrawals) during the period. Joseph Dietz in 1966 modified the formula to incorporate cash flows, but his approach is not exact. The Time Weighted Return method accommodates cash flows exactly---by circumventing all of them! Finally, the Internal Rate of Return method accommodates all cash flows and their dates! All methods can give different values and they do have different meanings. Which method should you use to assess the management of your savings or retirement accounts? This book has the answer for you.

Finally, we illuminate SEC definition of Total Return. Compare your total return to that of others!

This book teaches the reader the equations behind all methods mentioned and instructs on the construction of a spreadsheet. Alternately, Excel spreadsheets may be obtained from the author's email address. Finally, the reader's stock broker may have the methods installed on company computers, and will provide help in accessing and using them. For all alternatives, this book provides insight into each method and its interpretation.

TABLE OF CONTENTS

TABLE OF FIGURES

Measuring Investment Performance

1.   WHO NEEDS THIS BOOK

You have investment accounts holding stocks, bonds, certificates of deposit, mutual funds, exchange traded funds (ETFs), or money market funds. These accounts may be a brokerage account, an IRA, a Roth IRA, or a 401(k). Some are managed professionally, some are managed by you. Your manager selects securities to buy and sell and charges a fee. Maybe you manage an account for yourself and save the fee. How well is the manager or you doing?

This question arises even if your account consists of one stock and a money market fund to handle distributed cash. That account reports its market value daily and publishes a record of all deposits and withdrawals made by you. You can ask: How well is that account doing?

The account value increased this year, but maybe that was due to the extra funds that you deposited. Possibly, the account value decreased, but maybe that was due to the funds that you withdrew. How can one discover the rate of return of an investment account, without the impact of deposits or withdrawals? *That* rate of return assesses account management. It is different from account rate of growth which includes deposits and withdrawals.

Investment accounts are describable by their annual rates of return, their volatility (risk), their annual income, and their liquidity (cash readily available). Account management may be constrained by liquidity requirements imposed on the account. For example, you might require the manager to have six months living expense available within 30 days of request. An account manager may select securities to fit your conservative risk profile or to generate income that you require. All these factors influence the rate of return. It is a complex task to compare the management of different accounts.

We will use account rate of return as our sole metric to compare accounts. But, you should be aware of the other dimensions (risk, income, and liquidity) to account value.

Knowing the account annual rate of return permits you to verify that its management meets your savings goal prior to retirement. Given your annual savings, you need a minimum rate of return to achieve the desired account size by the year of retirement. When retired, you need a minimum rate of return in the account to meet its longevity goal. The account must outlast your life. Put another way, will you outlast your savings?

I faced these questions. I must withdraw funds from my IRA to support my retirement. In fact, the government mandates withdrawals because the account is a pretax IRA and I am older than 70-1/2 years. I manage this account. How do I assess my management of my IRA?

The withdrawals go into a standard brokerage account from which I write checks for living expenses. This account experiences multiple deposits and withdrawals, all made with irregular amounts and at irregular times. It also holds securities. I manage it myself. How do I assess my management of this account?

Mutual funds and exchange traded funds assess themselves by the "Total Return" published for the last one, three and five year periods. One desires to compare the management of your account to their total return values. Did you do as well as that stock fund or not? Perhaps you should invest in that fund and have them manage your account?

Joseph Dietz faced this question in 1966: How to assess the investment management of pension funds in the presence of extensive deposits and withdrawals. Deposits come from monthly payments by pensioners, and withdrawals come from benefits paid to pensioners. Chapter 3 describes his equation giving Return on Investment for this situation.

Chapter 4 describes the *Time-Weighted Rate of Return* (TWR) method. It computes account growth while excluding the effect of cash flows. This assesses account management which includes security selection, time of purchase and time of sales. It is used to assess management of retirement accounts because of their extensive cash flows. Its metric is the growth of $1000 over a period of time if dividends and interest are reinvested. This permits comparison to stock funds, but cannot evaluate how much money you have made or lost.

Chapter 5 describes the *Internal Rate of Return* (IRR) method. It measures account growth with all cash flows considered. The use of the XIRR function in Excel is explained. Chapter 7 compares TWR and IRR evaluations, giving an example where fortunate and unfortunate cash flows were detected by their IRR whereas the TWR value remained zero!

Methods are presented for you to apply TWR or IRR analysis to your account. Chapter 4 describes a spreadsheet that permits easy migration from your account records to the inputs required for a TWR analysis. Chapter 6 explains how to use the XIRR function in Excel spreadsheets to find the IRR of your retirement accounts. Alternatively, I can email the spreadsheets to you. Finally, your broker probably has these programs on company computers and will permit you to use them to evaluate your account.

Chapter 8 presents the Securities and Exchange Commission (SEC) definition of Total Return and explains why the TWR metric should be used to quantify the total return of your investment account. Proviso: Account charges identified by the SEC must be introduced. This permits comparison between the Total Return of your accounts and the Total Returns of mutual funds and exchange traded funds.

Chapters 9, 10 and 11 explain how this material is used to assess your savings account building up to the required retirement savings goal and the retirement account being slowly dissipated during retirement. Assessment before retirement means finding the rate of return achieved in savings and comparing it to the return required to meet your savings goal. Assessment during retirement involves finding the achieved rate of return and the resultant account longevity or "how long will the money last?" The TWR method is used to evaluate your achieved return.

I have taught Algebra and Statistics at Santa Barbara City College for eleven years.[1] My style is to explain concepts through examples. This approach will give you a fundamental understanding of the topics of this book I reference many web sites that explain the concepts in this booklet but I trust that my explanations will be more enlightening.

Return on Investment (ROI) is a simple concept (Chapter 2). It is the ratio of the increase (or decrease) in account value by the end of a period of time divided by its value at the beginning of the period. This simple formula is correct where no account deposits or withdrawals are made during the period. Where deposits or withdrawals occur, the account values at the beginning and end of the time period are meaningless by themselves. In this case, one must use the Dietz, TWR or IRR method to compute an annual rate of return. But, their values have different meanings, as explained therein.

Dietz, TWR and IRR methods reduce to the simple ROI formula for accounts with no deposits or withdrawals. In this sense they are consistent with each other.

The user will find many explanations at www.wikipedia.org and www.FINRA.org. Also see the following two Barron's Business Guides: Dictionary of Banking Terms, Thomas P. Fitch, and Dictionary of Accounting Terms, Shim and Siegel, CPA. Both are fifth edition. The Glossary in this book defines all acronyms and symbols used.

I welcome all comments and questions. Email me at nesteggcd@verizon.net

---

[1] The author received an MS degree (mathematics) in 1966 from the University of Washington..

2. AN INVESTMENT ACCOUNT--- ITS WITHDRAWALS, DEPOSITS, AND ROI

We define an investment account as one that holds a variety of securities, such as stocks, stock funds, bonds, bond funds, and has a money market fund to hold dividends, interest, and cash deposited by the owner. Fees and brokerage commissions are paid out of account assets. The account has a market value at the beginning and end of any time period, typically months or quarters. Examples encompass a brokerage account holding many types of securities down to an account holding stock from one company and a money market fund. We measure the investment performance of the aggregate account.

Account management involves selecting securities and times of their purchase or sale. It includes cash management---how much to hold in a money market fund and when to purchase other securities. Change in account value serves to assess account management. If no funds were added to or subtracted from the account during an assessment period, return on investment is calculated as:

RETURN ON INVESTMENT *(ROI)* =

$$\frac{account\ value\ at\ end\ of\ period - account\ value\ at\ beginning\ of\ period}{account\ value\ at\ beginning\ of\ period}$$

Or: $$ROI = \frac{investment\ return\ during\ period}{account\ value\ at\ beginning\ of\ period}$$

The account value at beginning of period is considered the investment. ROI is, literally, the return on investment. However, if funds were added during the period, are they also part of the investment? How are they incorporated in the equation? Possibly, a good ROI value for the period may be totally due to the added funds and not due to growth in value of securities held.

Also, if funds were withdrawn during the period, are they also part of the return realized? How are they incorporated in the equation? Possibly, a negative investment return is due to the withdrawal and not to declining securities value.

This conundrum is illustrated by the following three scenarios. All have an account beginning value of $1000. The account ending value at one year later is tabulated.

Scenario	Deposit at mid year	Account Ending value	Annual Investment return	Management assessment
1	$0	$1100	10% (ROI method)	Good
2	$100	$1100	0%	Poor
3	$100	$1200	9.53% (IRR method)	Best

The first scenario had no funds added. The simple ROI equation computes a 10% per year value. The second scenario had a deposit midyear so one is at a loss how to apply the simple ROI equation. But note: The ending account value is simply the sum of the beginning account value and the midyear deposit. Thus, there was no investment growth in the account! The investment return is zero. Although the account grew by 10%, the account manager did a poor job. The third scenario has an elevated ending value, presumably from astute account management. The investment return is 9.53%, although the account grew by 20%. I emphasize: *Account growth is different from investment return.* This book will teach how to compute investment returns in all situations.

The ROI equation does give the fractional change in account value in an assessment period even in the presence of cash flows. It cannot represent an ROI value if funds, external to account management purposes are withdrawn or added to the account during the time period. In such cases, other methodology must be used. However, **the ROI equation is fundamental to all methodologies.** You will see that all methodologies use this equation.

Examples of withdrawals are discretionary withdrawals for living expenses, withdrawals transferring funds to another account, or government mandated Minimum Required

Distributions (MRD) when owners of a pre-tax Individual Retirement Account reach 70-1/2 years of age. Examples of deposits are funds added from savings gleaned from employment or transfers from another account. Dividends which accumulate in the account are neither withdrawals nor deposits, but are part of account growth.

Our account evaluations will be pre-tax because every one's tax situation is different. Thus, deposits must be the net funds that enter the account. Taxes paid to make the deposit are outside the purview of the account and are ignored. Funds withdrawn from the account must be gross amounts, including taxes withheld. The pre-tax assessment will describe account behavior independent of taxes.

If one has an Individual Retirement Account (IRA) with required minimum distributions (MRDs), the brokerage account will suggest withholding an amount for income taxes. You will receive a net distribution, but you must record the gross distribution as a withdrawal.

Income generated by the account (dividends and interest) are not additions but are returns on investment, provided the funds remain in the cash repository and thus grow account value. If these funds are withdrawn to fund living expense or transfer to another account, then these funds are withdrawals.

A loan from the broker to purchase stocks on margin is not an addition.[2] The added cash is balanced by an added liability (the loan) and the net account value (market value of holdings minus the loan) is unchanged, except for fees involved. When stocks are sold and the loan repaid, the repayment is not a withdrawal because the repayment does not change the account net value. In other words, use the net account value to calculate ROI in a margin account. Net account value is the owner's equity.

The remainder of this book explains how others have addressed the problem of computing ROI in the presence of cash flow, either withdrawals or deposits. The Glossary explains all acronyms and symbols used.

---

[2] A margin account with a brokerage firm enables a customer to borrow money for additional transactions, using securities owned and deposited with the firm as collateral or margin for additional purchases. Margin is the amount of money the customer must deposit. [Fitch, FINRA] The net account value equals market value minus the borrowed funds and accrued unpaid interest.

3.   THE DIETZ MODIFICATION OF THE ROI EQUATION

The simple ROI equation cannot evaluate account return in the presence of uncontrolled cash flows during the evaluation period. Pension funds especially, experience multiple deposits (payments to the pension fund) and withdrawals (payments to pensioners) every month. In his classic work, Dietz addressed the problem of computing Rates of Return of Pension Funds.[3] In describing his model he says: "This assumes contributions are received midway through each investment period, and alternatively, that half the contributions are received at the beginning of the period, and half at the end of the period."[4] We derive his equation using the latter idea.

His original work is primarily of historical significance because the widespread use of computers now permits complicated analyses such as the Time-Weighted Return and the Internal Rate of Return methods. These do not suffer the assumptions of the Dietz method. The Dietz equations are presented because his method of *incorporating* deposits and withdrawals into the ROI equation is the same as used by the TWR method to *sidestep* deposits and withdrawals. Thus, examining his approach enables the understanding of the TWR method to be treated in the next chapter.

Dietz was aware of limitation of his model of contributions as these quotes from page 66 indicate. "Rates of return were developed on a quarterly basis from the formula developed in chapter IV." Footnote: "Quarterly periods were used because…the assumption that fund inflows and outflows occur at midpoint is untenable for a yearly period."

---

[3] Dietz, Peter O. *Pension Funds: Measuring Investment Performance*. Free Press, 1966.
[4] Dietz, Page 51

To derive his equation, define these symbols:

> AVS = account value at start of the period, before all cash flows
> AVE = account value at end of the period, after all cash flows
> W = Withdrawals made during the period
> D = Deposits made during the period

 If only withdrawals occurred from the account, half are deemed to occur just after beginning of the period and half are deemed to occur just prior to the end of the period. Thus the starting funds available to grow during the period are: AVS-W/2. The account value near the end of the period attains AVE+W/2 before the withdrawal reduces it to AVE. The investment growth in the account is (AVE+W/2) – (AVS-W/2). The formula for ROI is then:

$$ROI = \frac{(AVE + W/2) - (AVS - W/2)}{AVS - W/2}$$

$$ROI = \frac{AVE - AVS + W}{AVS - W/2}$$

If only deposits occurred to the account, D/2 deposited near the beginning of the period will add to the account value at the start and grow at the ROI for the period. The D/2 deposited near the end of the period will not grow at the ROI for the period and must be subtracted from the account value at the end of the period. The formula for ROI becomes:

$$ROI = \frac{(AVE - D/2) - (AVS + D/2)}{AVS + D/2}$$

$$ROI = \frac{AVE - AVS - D}{AVS + D/2}$$

Let C denote the net cash flow during the period. Define it as: **C = D – W.** The above equations can be combined to read:

$$R = \frac{AVE - AVS - C}{AVS + 0.5C}$$

This is Dietz's equation 4.6.

The Modified Dietz Method performs a more careful determination of the invested capital. The 0.5C term in the denominator is replaced by a more careful calculation of when the contributions took place within the period of evaluation. See the Wikipedia article on this subject.[5]

The TWR method solves the cash flow problem by conforming holding periods to the cash flow. You no longer need to worry about where cash flows will be placed. They are placed exactly on their dates of occurrence and where they can be exactly circumvented. The time-weighted return evaluates the account as if no cash flows occurred. This is the return due solely to growth in investments.

The IRR method includes all cash flows and their dates of occurrence for calculating the Internal Rate of Return. This evaluates account growth including the effects of all cash flows. Chapter 5 explains this.[6]

Charles Schwab and Co. and other firms provide both methodologies for clients to adjudge the performance of their accounts. Chapter 7 compares all methodologies and provides an example to illustrate their differences.

---

[5] http://en.wikipedia.org/wiki/Modified_Dietz_Method

[6] See site www.mhj3.com/pc_help/Dietz_calculation1.htm for a discussion of Dietz, TWR, and IRR methods. For another good explanation of TWR and IRR visit: www.merriman.com

4.   THE METHOD OF TIME-WEIGHTED RETURN[7]

The discussion thus far assumed that a fixed holding period is imposed--- one month, one quarter or one year, and ROI must be calculated for the period, somehow incorporating the cash flows that occurred during the period. The problems of this approach go away if holding periods are tailored to the cash flows. The only rule is that **holding periods end with every cash flow---the cash flow occurs on the last day of the period.**[8] The duration of variable holding periods are controlled by the owner and are unpredictable, but each holding period can have an exact assessment of its ROI. This approach is called Time-Weighted-Returns. If holding periods are one day, it is called Daily TWR.

Cash flows are funds, either deposited or withdrawn from the account. Dividends, interest payments, and capital gains converted to cash, and which accumulate in the account are not cash flows. They are part of account investment growth which is measured by the methods described in this book.

The equations for the TWR method are provided to give the reader insight on how cash flows are sidestepped. Thus, only investments growth (or decline) is calculated. The reader may eschew the algebra and use the software available at his broker. The equations will give insight as how the TWR method avoids all cash flows.

---

[7] www.investopedia.com/exam-guide/cfa-level-1/
Look at tab /quantitative-methods/. Section 2.7 titled Money vs. Time-Weighted Return.

If a holding period is ended by a withdrawal, the withdrawal must be added back to the account ending value in order to assess account growth during the holding period. Thus, the ROI for the holding period is:

$$ROI = \frac{AVE + W - AVS}{AVS}$$

AVE is the value after the withdrawal and is the proper AVS for the subsequent holding period.

Suppose the holding period is ended by a deposit, meaning that the deposit occurred on the last day of the period. The deposit did not contribute to account growth and is not part of the ROI. Thus, we remove the deposit from the account ending value to find the ROI for the holding period. The ROI for the holding period is:

$$ROI = \frac{AVE - D - AVS}{AVS}$$

AVE includes the deposit and is the proper AVS for the subsequent period.

We combine these two equations to cover the general case where deposits and withdrawals may occur on the same day and terminate a holding period:

$$ROI = \frac{AVE + W - D - AVS}{AVS}$$

Note that W and D can be zero. Thus one may terminate a holding period at any time, even without cash flows. You might terminate at the end of every month when account statements arrive and the account market value is reported. However, such holding periods must be included in TWR evaluation.

The equation can be rewritten as:

$$1 + ROI = \frac{AVE + W - D}{AVS}$$

We refer to "1+ROI" as the multiplier for the holding period. An investment made at the beginning of the holding period will have its value increased (or decreased) by 1+ROI. For example, if ROI was 10% during the holding period, $1000 at the beginning becomes (1+0.1) × $1000 = $1100 at the end.

These equations give the exact ROI for a holding period. ROI is generally desired for standard periods, one month, one quarter, or one year. These periods will likely hold many holding periods. Suppose we use one year as the encompassing period. How can one assess the ROI for one year? No funds can be identified that are either the investment or return, that were present throughout the year and whose growth can be assessed by the end of the year to form the basis of an ROI computation.

The concept used, is to consider each holding period in the year as a separate crap shoot. Each has its own ROI. The user takes the funds from one crap shoot (labeled AVE) and inputs them to the subsequent crap shoot (labeled AVS). The values of AVS change with each crap shoot because of the prior crap shoot gain or loss and cash input or output. Any funds that are present at the start of the year and remain in the account to the end of the year will grow by the boost (or decline) offered by each crap shoot. The increase or decline offered by all the crap shoots is the product of their "1+ROI" values.

Because there were many investments and withdrawals throughout the year, one cannot compute a dollar gain or loss for the year. The terminology of Return on Investment (ROI) is not used to describe an account. The growth over the year of an arbitrary amount, generally $10,000, is used to describe account growth. This is TWR data. However, ROI is appropriate to describe each holding period because there is only one investment in a holding period---the account starting value (AVS).

Let *ROI* (j) denote the ROI for the jth holding period in the year. The multiplier for the year is the product of the multipliers of all holding periods: [9]

$$Multiplier = \prod_j(1 + ROI(j))$$

Let R denotes the return for the year. Then the multiplier for the year is 1+R where:

$$1 + R = \prod_j(1 + ROI(j))$$

And $R = \prod_j(1 + ROI(j)) - 1$

This is the Time-Weighted Return for the year. It is the composite of all ROIs encountered and is not affected by the intervening cash flows. It measures only the market gains or losses and thus can assess account management, referring to stock selection for purchase or sale.

However, do not blame your account manager for account declines when the overall market declines. Your account might be compared to some benchmarks to properly assess management. However, the R value obtained is a fact for your financial analysis.

Account growth through the year is a separate book keeping calculation contained in the account summary report provided by the broker. The fractional growth may be more or less than the R value provided by TWR analysis. Account growth is influenced by cash flows whereas R is not.

The next page contains a photograph of an Excel spreadsheet that embodies the equations for Time Weighted Return. The data illustrates a typical account. Every date and market value with or without a cash flow terminates a holding period. (Note: The first entry, on 12/28/2012, does not terminate a holding period. It begins the first holding period and is required.) Blue cells contain user input. TWR equations are in the column labeled "Holding

---

[9] The glossary describes these algebra symbols.

Period Multipliers". Multipliers are calculated at the ending date of each holding period. Equations are provided to enable one to construct the spreadsheet. Alternatively, you may order the spreadsheet by emailing me at nesteggCD@verizon.net. I will email it back.

The blue cells are for user data. First, input all dates with cash flows and account market values as illustrated. Dates without cash flows are acceptable, but market values are required. Do not skip lines. Then alter the red cell that instructs the range of multipliers (and dates) to consider. The return for those dates is computed.

The spreadsheet computes 17.09% time-weighted return for the year. But what was the dollar gain? Here is a simple answer. Through the year, the owner had invested $90580.24 + $7354.07 = $97934.31. At the end of the year, the owner could or had withdrawn $110500 + $3147.17 = $113647.17. The dollar gain is $15712.86 or 16.0% of the total investment.

TWR is an unequivocal evaluation of account management. It assesses account growth without the effects of cash flows. The IRR method computes the account rate of growth and includes the effects of cash flows. We treat it next.

CALCULATION OF TIME-WEIGHTED RATE OF RETURN — Figure in Chapter 4.

Row	Column B HOLDING PERIOD ENDING DATES	Column C DEPOSITS	Column D WITHDRAWALS	Column E ACCOUNT VALUES AT END OF DAY	Column F HOLDING PERIOD MULTIPLIERS
4					#VALUE!
5					#DIV/0!
6	12/28/2012	$90,580.24		$90,580.24	#DIV/0!
7	1/4/2013	$1,462.27		$96,006.52	1.0438
8	1/11/2013			$95,557.59	0.9953
9	1/20/2013	$422.75		$97,131.87	1.0121
10	1/25/2013		$1,400.00	$96,321.33	1.0061
11	2/1/2013			$97,403.00	1.0112
12	2/9/2013	$1,682.10	$567.17	$98,805.62	1.0030
13	2/17/2013		$300.00	$99,907.76	1.0142
14	3/1/2013			$100,878.79	1.0097
15	3/8/2013	$1,682.10		$105,094.04	1.0251
16	3/16/2013			$106,538.83	1.0137
17	3/29/2013		$600.00	$107,417.89	1.0139
18	4/6/2013	$1,682.10	$280.00	$108,728.41	0.9991
19	4/12/2013			$111,245.25	1.0231
20	4/19/2013	$422.75		$109,918.42	0.9843
21	4/26/2013			$111,410.24	1.0136
22	4/30/2013			$112,793.79	1.0124
23	12/28/2013			$110,500.00	0.9797
24					0.0000
					#DIV/0!
					#DIV/0!

INSTRUCTIONS: Enter your account data in the blue cells. Do not skip lines. Holding periods extend from one date to the date on the next line. Each line must have a date and account value. Dates without cash flows are permitted. Account values denote the end of holding periods. Example: the multiplier formula in cell F8 is =(E8-C8+D8)/E7. To select the return for a different time period, alter the Excel code in the red cell below. Code format: =PRODUCT(F7:F23) generates the product of multipliers in column F from rows 7 through 23.

Product of multipliers =	1.1709
ROI for selected period =	17.09%

5.   INTERNAL RATE OF RETURN (IRR)

IRR is another method of evaluating the growth of an investment account over a given time period. It considers the account values at the beginning and end of the period, all intervening cash flows and their times from start to end. Unlike TWR method, it does not use intervening account values. Any time period for assessment can be used, but one year is standard. We will use one year. [10]

IRR seems to be an all encompassing methodology so you would wish to have its equations for programming and use. Unfortunately its equations are complex and cannot be solved explicitly for IRR. One must work through iteration. That means, insert a trial value for IRR and see if that solves the equation. If it does not, use another trial value. Hundreds of trial values may be required before a value is found that solves the equation to suitable accuracy.

In any case, the Excel function XIRR does this iteration for you and absolves the reader from the algebra. We will instruct the use of XIRR after we explain the meaning of IRR.

First take the easy situation of no cash flows throughout the year. Suppose one has $10000 at the start of the year and $11000 at the end. Obviously we gained 10% for the year. The gain is assumed to consist of 365 equal daily returns on investment. This idea of equal daily return values is fundamental to IRR. Now, for a little algebra….

Let G denote the daily return on investment. After the first day the account value is $10000*(1+G). After two days the account value is $10000*(1+G)*(1+G). After 365 days the account value is $10000*(1+G)^{365}$. This must equal $11000. This equation can be solved for G:

---

[10] It is also called Money-Weighted Return. See Chapter 2.7 of CFA Level 1 exam guide at WWW.investopedia.com.

$$G = \left(\frac{11000}{10000}\right)^{1/365} - 1$$

This G is the daily Internal Rate of Return. Its value for this example is 0.02612% per day.

In reality, daily ROI values fluctuate up and down, but they connect the ending value AVE to the starting value AVS. The value of G is termed their geometric mean. It is a plausible daily ROI value that connects the AVS and AVE values [11]

Now we introduce a withdrawal of $100 on, say, day 37 of the year. Cash flows are assumed to occur at the end of the day after market gains for the day. This will be the sole cash flow in this example to illustrate how G is determined. The value of the account at the close of day 37 is:

$10000*(1+G)^{37}$ - $100

This value then grows by $(1+G)^{328}$ for the balance of the year. The value at year end must equal $11000. The equation for G is:

[$10000*(1+G)^{37}$ -$100]*$(1+G)^{328}$ = $11000.

Just one cash flow results in a complex equation![12] Imagine what several cash flows throughout the year would do!

We use the XIRR function to solve this equation. The result is: G=0.02884% per day or 11.10% per year.[13] That single withdrawal on day 37 has increased the yearly internal rate of

---

[11] See the Wikipedia entry on Geometric Mean. (en.wikipedia.org/wiki/Geometric_mean)

[12] This equation is called a polynomial of degree 328. It is not solvable algebraically for G.
[13] The XIRR evaluation produces more decimal places. For simplicity we use only four significant figures.

return from 10% to 11.1%. This arises from the decreased account value on day 37 that must gain more per day to achieve the ending account value of $11000.

To demonstrate that G=0.0002884 solves the equation; we insert it into the left side of the equation. The result of a hand calculation is $10999.97. This equals $11000 approximately. If we had used more decimal places for G our fit would be exact.

If the $100 withdrawal occurred on some other day, say day 110, the numbers 37 and 328 become respectively, 110 and 255. This is a mathematically different equation. Its solution is G=0.0002878 and IRR value of 11.08% per year. While not a dramatic change in IRR in this example, it demonstrates that XIRR values are fundamentally sensitive to the dates of cash flows.

In brief, the daily IRR value is a number G that connects the account ending value to its beginning value, including all funds that were in the account at some time. The Internal Rate of Return for the year is obtained from that daily value by the equation:

$$IRR = (1 + G)^{365} - 1$$

The Excel function XIRR does this calculation

6.   USE OF THE XIRR FUNCTION

Select a cell in which the value of XIRR should appear. Code that cell as: = XIRR (cash flow array, date array). For "date array" list the rows containing dates of all cash flows. Dates without cash flows are accepted. Suppose your dates are in rows 6 through 23 of column B as in the following figure. The date array entry would then be B6:B23. The colon tells Excel that all values between those rows are used. The XIRR function is designed to compute the IRR value for a year. The dates in column B must encompass one year or more.

The following figure is a spreadsheet for calculating IRR from cash flow data in column E. The "cash flow array" would then be: E6:E23. The cash flow and date arrays must use corresponding rows. In conclusion, the XIRR cell coding is:

> = XIRR (E6:E23, B6:B23)

The equal sign is required. The value appears in the XIRR cell.

The user inputs his data in columns B, C and D The software computes the daily net cash flow in column E as: "withdrawals minus deposits". The starting value in a period ($90,580.24) is entered as a deposit and the ending value ($110,500.00) as a withdrawal. The user inputs the record of deposits and withdrawals and the software computes the cash flow. Examine the figure to see how these considerations are implemented.

XIRR computes the annual Internal Rate-of Return. The first and last dates should be one or more years apart.

The spreadsheet computes 16.71% Internal Rate of Return. This includes the effects of all cash flows. This annual return is close to the 17.09% growth computed using the TWR methodology. Chapter 7 presents examples where the methodologies can give totally different evaluations.

CALCULATION OF IRR BETWEEN TWO DATES

Row	Column B DATES	Column C DEPOSITS	Column D WITHDRAWALS	Column E CASH FLOW FOR DAY
4				
5				
6	12/28/2012	$90,580.24		-$90,580.24
7	1/4/2013	$1,462.27		-$1,462.27
8	1/11/2013			$0.00
9	1/20/2013	$422.75		-$422.75
10	1/25/2013		$1,400.00	$1,400.00
11	2/1/2013			$0.00
12	2/9/2013	$1,682.10	$567.17	-$1,114.93
13	2/17/2013		$300.00	$300.00
14	3/1/2013			$0.00
15	3/8/2013	$1,682.10		-$1,682.10
16	3/16/2013			$0.00
17	3/29/2013		$600.00	$600.00
18	4/6/2013	$1,682.10	$280.00	-$1,402.10
19	4/12/2013			$0.00
20	4/19/2013	$422.75		-$422.75
21	4/26/2013			$0.00
22	4/30/2013			$0.00
23	12/28/2013		$110,500.00	$110,500.00
24				

XIRR(E6:E23,B6:B23) =	16.71%	per year.

Instructions: Do not skip lines between dates. XIRR translates all data to a one-year period. To obtain a IRR per year, the dates must span one year or more..

7.   COMPARISON OF METHODOLOGIES

The IRR methodology uses all cash flow data and their dates of occurrence, and the starting and ending market values for the assessment period, generally one year. The methodology finds a single daily ROI value that connects starting and ending account values, while accounting for all cash flows. That value is the geometric mean of the actual daily ROI values. The annual IRR value is computed from the mean daily ROI value. Only starting and ending market values are required---intervening values are not used.

The TWR methodology does not employ the geometric mean idea, but employs the idea of sequential crap shoots to evaluate account fractional return through the year. The percentage gain or loss is calculated for each crap shoot. The amount of funds at stake in each crap shoot will vary but that does not affect the percentage gain or loss value. But it prevents one from computing the dollar gain or loss. The TWR methodology gives an exact assessment of rate of return for funds that are present throughout the year. For this reason the TWR methodology should be used when comparing management of different accounts. Stock funds describe their performance with a chart showing the growth of $1 or $10,000 over a 1, 3, or 5 year period. This is TWR data.

The best way to exhibit method differences is by using them to analyze a simple but realistic account. We show two cases: a fortunate cash flow and an unfortunate cash flow. The following table shows the activities in one quarter for the fortunate cash flow. On February 1 the individual sold ten shares of stock at a market high and withdrew the $1100. On March 1 he/she purchased twenty shares at a market low, using an $1800 deposit. Brokerage commissions are omitted. No dividends were paid. The account value increased 10% for the quarter.

Transaction Dates	Stock price	Transaction	Shares owned	Owner's Cash Flow	Account value at end of day
1/1/2012	$100		100	0	$10000
2/1/2012	$110	Sold 10 shares at $110	90	+$ 1100	$ 9900
3/1/2012	$90	Purchased 20 shares at $90	110	-$ 1800	$ 9900
3/31/2012	$100		110	0	$11000

First, compute the Time Weighted Return for the quarter. There are three holding periods. The first ends with a withdrawal on Feb. 1. The multiplier equation is:

$$1 + ROI = \frac{AVE + W}{AVS}$$

The values are: AVE = $9900, AVS = $10000 and W = $1100. The multiplier is 1.1 (ROI = 0.1).

The second holding period ends with a deposit on March 1. Its multiplier equation is:

$$1 + ROI = \frac{AVE - D}{AVS}$$

The values are: AVE = $9900, AVS = $9900, D = $1800 and the multiplier equals 0.8182 (ROI = -0.1818). This is a loss of 18 %.

The third holding period ends March 31 with no cash flows, but the stock increased in price. The multiplier is:

$$1 + ROI = \frac{AVE}{AVS}$$

The values are: AVE = $11000, AVS = $9900 and the multiplier equals 1.1111. (Price increase = 11.1%) The multiplier for the quarter is: 1.1*0.8182*1.1111 = 1.0000.

(Calculations are rounded off to four decimal places.) The time weighted return for the quarter is zero. This corresponds to the fact that the stock price at the end was the same as at the start. Thus, there would be no gain for funds that were fully invested through the quarter. However, the owner realized a dollar gain of $11000-$10000-$1800+$1100 = +$300.

Dividends paid are not deposits. They are added to the account values and are part of account gains. They are not withdrawals unless actually withdrawn from the account. This example had no dividends paid.

The following table shows account activities with unfortunate cash flows. The individual bought ten shares at a market high, using $1100 of deposited funds, then sold 20 shares at a low and withdrew the $1800.

Transaction Dates	Stock Price	Transaction	Shares owned	Owner's Cash Flow	Account value at end of day
1/1/12	$100		100	0	$10000
2/1/12	$110	Purchased 10 shares at $110	110	-$ 1100	$12100
3/1/12	$ 90	Sold 20 shares at $90	90	+$ 1800	$ 8100
3/31/12	$100		90	0	$ 9000

The first holding period ends with a deposit on Feb. 1. Its data is: AVE = $12100, AVS = $10000 and D = $1100. Its multiplier value is: 1.1. The second holding period ends with a withdrawal on March 1. Its data is: AVE=$8100, AVS=$12100 and W=$1800. Its multiplier value is 0.8182. The third holding period ends March 31 with no cash flow. Its data is: AVE = $9000 and AVS = $8100. It multiplier value is 1.1111. The product of three multiplier values is 1.0000, rounding off to four decimal places. Thus, there was zero time-weighted return for the quarter. The reason is that the stock price ended at the same value as it began. However, the owner lost $9000 - $10000 - $1100 + $1800 = -$300.

Thus, the TWR methodology computes no difference between the two accounts. Both exhibit zero time-weighted return on investment for the quarter. To repeat: The TWR method is sensitive to only market gain. It assesses the account with the influence of cash flows removed. It does not compute the dollar gain or loss resulting from cash flows.

However, the Internal Rate of Return (using XIRR) for the fortunate cash flow is 12.90% per annum. This amounts to 3.08% per quarter. A simple calculation verifies this figure. Over the three months, the owner deposited $11800 into the account and withdrew $12100. His return is $300 on the $10000 investment. This is about three percent over three months. The IRR method computes the dollar gain or loss.

XIRR for the unfortunate cash flow is: -11.49 % per annum, or -3.05 % per quarter. A simple calculation verifies this figure. During the quarter the owner deposited $11100 and withdrew $10800 at the end. This is a loss of $300 in the quarter or three percent of the original investment.

What would Peter Dietz say? We repeat his equation:

$$R = \frac{AVE - AVS - C}{AVS + 0.5C}$$

The following table shows the R calculated for the two cash flow cases. R is the ROI for the quarter. The Dietz equation is consistent with the XIRR values for these two simple cases. It is sensitive to cash flows.

Cash Flow	AVE	AVS	C	R
Fortunate	$11000	$10000	$700	2.90%
Unfortunate	$ 9000	$10000	-$700	-3.11%

The TWR value insulates the account manager from uncontrollable cash flows. TWR assesses the market induced growth (or declines) on the portfolio and is not influenced by the magnitude or timing of cash flows. That is why it is used to assess the account manager skill at selection of investments. However, a TWR value of 0% does not assess what happened to the investor in terms of dollar profit or loss. Fortunate or astute cash flows may generate much profit, as in the above example. Internal Rate of Return (IRR) will assess the investment performance for the investor.[14] The Dietz equation is a fast way to approximately assess return on investment. It should be used for quarterly periods.

In the absence of cash flows, all methods give the same ROI as the basic equation presented in Chapter 2. In this sense they are consistent with each other. On the other hand, TWR and IRR calculations are unnecessary in the absence of cash flows. The simple equation for ROI will suffice.

A low value to TWR may be due to a general market decline rather than to poor account management. However, the TWR value is a real marker as to account growth. This is treated in Chapter 9.

---

[14] An excellent discussion of TWR and IRR is given in the web site:
//en.wikipedia.org/wiki/True_Time-Weighted_Rate_of_Return

8.   FINDING YOUR TOTAL RETURN

Should you manage your investment account or should you convert it to a mutual fund or exchange traded fund (ETF) and have someone else manage the account? Wikipedia describes these funds in detail. Their performance is given as the growth of $10,000 over a several year period. This is TWR data. We confine this discussion to comparing the rates of return available from each option.

Total Return is defined by the Securities and Exchange Commission (SEC) in Form N-1A. The following paragraphs are quotes from the publication.[15]

"Form N-1A is to be used by open-end investment companies…to provide investors with information that will assist them in making a decision about investing in an investment company eligible to use the form."

Form N-1A is organized into 35 items. Item 26 of the form is titled Calculation of Performance Data. Section (b) of that item presents the formula for Average Annual Total Return. It equates the initial amount invested to the ending redeemable value, according to the following formula:

(Quote) $P(1+T)^N = ERV$

Where: P =   A hypothetical initial payment of $1000.

T =   average annual total return

N =   number of years

---

[15] Form N-1A, U.S. Securities and Exchange Commission/ home page. SEC 2052 (2-10). An open-ended investment company buys and sells shares from individual investors. The number of shares outstanding is not limited. Mutual Funds, Exchange Traded Funds and Money Market Funds are such companies.

ERV = Ending redeemable value of a hypothetical $1000 payment made at the beginning of the 1-, 5-, or 10-year periods at the end of the 1-, 5-, or 10- year periods (or fractional portion).

Instructions:

1. Assume the maximum sales load (or other charges) is deducted from the initial $1000 payment.

2. Assume all distributions by the fund are reinvested at the price stated in the prospectus (including any sales load imposed upon reinvestment of dividends) on the reinvestment dates during the period.

3. Include all reoccurring fees that are charged to all shareholder accounts. (Some details are here omitted.)

4. Determine the ending redeeming value by assuming a complete redemption at the end of the ...period, and the deduction of all nonrecurring charges deducted at the end of each period. (Some details are here omitted.)

(End quote)

This is the end of selections from the SEC note. The material presented here are for pretax calculations. The SEC note continues with after tax calculation. We omit that material.

SEC defines Total Return for the shareholder, as the difference between the ending redeemable value and the initial payment to the fund. If all SEC identified charges are made to your accounts, then their annual return will be comparable to published total return values. The only difference is the brokerage fees involved in starting up and in liquidating your account. These charges vary with the broker, whether the transaction is online or requires a human interface, and whether stocks, stock funds, and foreign securities are transacted. They can be as low as a fraction of percent of the transaction value. [16]

The SEC equation does not account for cash flows in your account. It implicitly assumes that the $1000 initial investment is all there is and remains in the account until the end of the period. Therefore, the TWR methodology is most appropriate for computing the Total Return of your investment account. If no cash flows occurred during the period of assessment, the simple equation for ROI can be used. Recall that all methods revert to the simple ROI equation in the absence of cash flows.

Your account management may not immediately reinvest dividends, but have them accumulate in the cash repository. Allowing dividends to accumulate without being reinvested is a conservative strategy. Had the dividends been immediately reinvested, their value would have been degraded by subsequent declines in the market price of securities. Alternatively, their value would have been enhanced if the market prices had subsequently increased. Allowing dividends to accumulate is a conservative strategy for dividend reinvestment. However, in a rising market your total return will be less than that of stock funds which manage to reinvest dividends as soon as they are paid.

Total return measures overall account management. If no income taxes are deducted from the account, then they are pretax evaluators. If taxes are withheld and withdrawn, then they are after tax evaluators.

A simple formula is available to estimate the total return of a brokerage account with no deposits or withdrawals and where dividends or interest are NOT reinvested but accrue as cash in the cash repository. In twelve months the account will accumulate the dividends, and

[16] Charles Schwab and Co. charges $8.95 for on-line transactions. This is 0.1% of an $8950 transaction. See their web site for details.

gain (or lose) value by its capital gain. (We ignore the small returns from cash invested in money markets.) The simple formula for total return is:

Total return for year = capital gain for year + total dividends paid in year

$$\text{Total ROI for year} = \frac{total\ return\ for\ year}{account\ value\ at\ beginning\ of\ year}$$

$$= \frac{capital\ gain\ for\ year}{(account\ value\ at\ beginning\ of\ year)} +$$

$$\frac{total\ dividends\ paid\ in\ year}{(account\ value\ at\ beginning\ of\ year)}$$

Total ROI for year = ROI due to capital gains + dividend yield of account.

This equation assumes that dividends accumulate for the year and are not reinvested. Total return for the year must use the ending redeemable value. Deduct the commissions required to redeem the account.

9. INTRODUCTION TO EVALUATING ROI NEEDS FOR RETIREMENT

The following two chapters' present charts illustrating the impact of rates of return upon savings account growth before retirement and savings account decline after retirement. Savings accounts before retirement tend to grow because of the periodic savings deposits. However, deposits may hide poor management. Savings tend to decline after retirement because one is steadily withdrawing funds for living expense. These withdrawals may overshadow good or poor account management. Account management is assessed by the annual TWR value of the account because this measure circumvents cash flow.[17] The annual rates of return used in the mathematics of the charts are TWR values.

Suppose after reading these chapters you decide that a rate of return of 6% per year is required to achieve your financial goals. What does this number mean and how can one tell if the retirement account is meeting this standard?

First consider a savings account building up to retirement.

You periodically deposit funds into the savings account. Suppose you make one deposit a year. We use the TWR convention of chapter 4; that is, holding periods last until the next deposit. The account should grow from its value just after the last deposit up to the value just after the next deposit one year hence. Subtract the second deposit from the year-end account value because it did not participate in market growth. The resulting net growth is solely due to market action and is the rate of return of the charts. This is a TWR value. Compare that return to the 6% value you require. If its growth equaled or exceeded 6% then your savings plan is on track. Note that account growth percentage includes the deposits and is likely much more than the TWR value.

---

[17] We remind you that a low TWR value may be due to overall market declines and not to poor management.

A TWR calculation evaluates account growth due solely to market action. This is the rate of return used in the charts. In the presence of multiple deposits (and withdrawals) in a year, use the TWR spreadsheet given in chapter 4, to assess account rate of return. Multiple deposits can cause the account to grow and hide poor management. Poor account management is a warning of future problems and should be discussed with your advisor. Ideally your TWR value will exceed the 6% requirement.[18]

Now consider the retirement account during retirement (chapter 11). Cash withdrawals during retirement may or may not overshadow market gains. The account could grow in the presence of withdrawals or it could decline. This behavior is normal. How can one assess management of this account?

The time-weighted return methodology will assess market gain or loss while sidestepping all cash flows. In a retirement account, the TWR value may exceed your 6% requirement even though account value declines. That is normal. The TWR values determine account longevity.

To assess your withdrawal size and account longevity, build the Excel spreadsheet in Chapter 11, titled "Verification of Account Longevity". Use the data specific to your situation. Your retirement account is in good shape if the TWR value exceeds 6% and the account longevity exceeds your expected life time.

---

[18] If no withdrawals were made from the savings account, its IRR value may be identical to the TWR value. It can be easier to compute IRR rather than TWR.

10.   ROI NEEDS WHEN SAVING FOR RETIREMENT

Many firms specialize in financial planning for retirement. The process is: first help the client to determine his desired lifestyle in retirement and the cost of that lifestyle. A fallback more austere lifestyle may also be defined. These costs include inflation of the cost of living until the retirement date. The annual cost is then multiplied to an amount that will likely last the life of the client. This is your retirement account goal.

The second step is to set up a savings plan to attain the retirement goal and an account to hold the funds. The third step is to acquire an advisor to manage the account. His job is to select investments that meet the risks profile of the client and attain the required rate of return.

This chapter examines the rates of return required of the savings account building up to attain the planned size at retirement. The next chapter treats the years in retirement to distribute the funds. It addresses account longevity, the years until it is all spent. In other words: to ensure that your assets outlive you.

The next three charts illustrate the role of investment return (R) in supporting your savings toward retirement. You may be just beginning your savings and have many years to go, or you may be older and have fewer years to go. Plots are provided to match the years until you retire.

Chart underpinnings are:

- Start with $100 deposited per month at the beginning of the first year.
- Each year increase deposits by 0%, 2% or 3% (due to cost-of-living raises).
- Deposits continue until retirement.
- Deposited funds grow at R% return each year

The charts show the savings accumulated for a given rate of return. The account ending value scales with the $100 deposit. For example, double the savings scale if you start with

$200 per month savings. Triple the scale if you start with $300 per month savings. The plots do not change.

Suppose you wish to retire in 30 years with $600,000 in the bank and you expect your salary to increase 2% annually. According to the 2% chart, starting your savings at $100 monthly and, given a 6% annual return on savings, will reap about $122,000 in 30 years. Thus, your monthly savings need to start at $100*(600/122) =$491.80 to meet your $600,000 goal. This amount saved is assumed to increase 2% each year in line with salary increases.

Another example: You wish to retire in 20 years and you have saved some, but you need $300,000 in additional retirement funds. You expect 3% annual pay raises. The 3% chart says at 6% annual return, $100 a month accumulates to $60,000. So, to achieve the $300,000, you have to begin saving $100*(300/60) =$500 per month for the next 20 years. This amount is assumed to increase 3% each year.

Third example: You plan to retire in 15 years with a pension. The pension just gets you by, but you like $4000 more income per year. Many large companies provide 4% dividends per year. Investing $100,000 in the stock of such companies would provide the $4000 extra income. The 2% chart indicates $100 saved per month at 6% investment return achieves $33000 in 15 years. Thus, saving $300 per month will achieve $100,000 in 15 years.

The years spent saving is more important than the ROI used. Consider the 30 year example. If you began saving five years earlier, your monthly savings could start at $100*(600/179) =$335.30 to meet your $600,000 goal. To achieve this goal in 30 years with that savings rate, a ROR of 8% is required. The graph with the 3% annual raise tells a similar story.

A rate of return of 6% is reasonable for a 30 year period, but one at 8% is speculative. The next chapter presents data on returns achievable in the equity stock market. It identifies what are conservative and speculative returns.

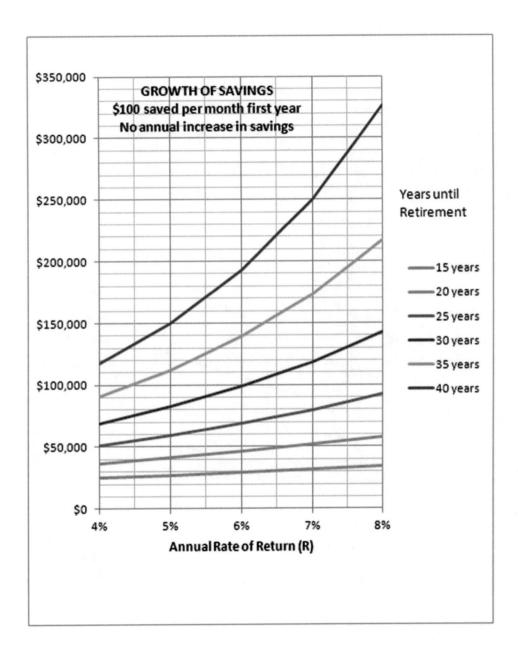

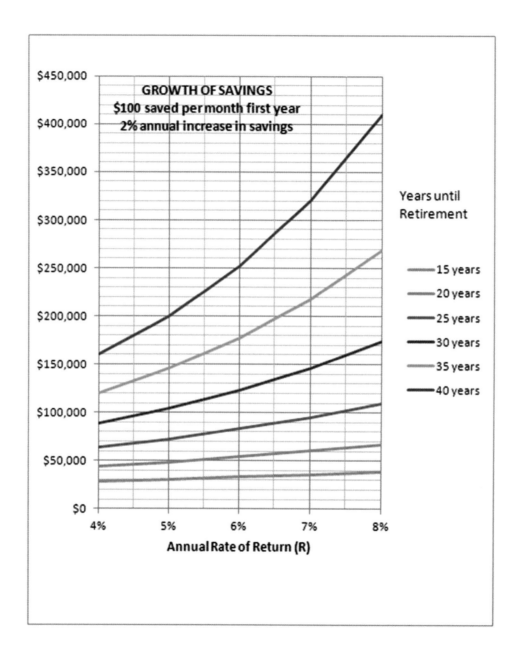

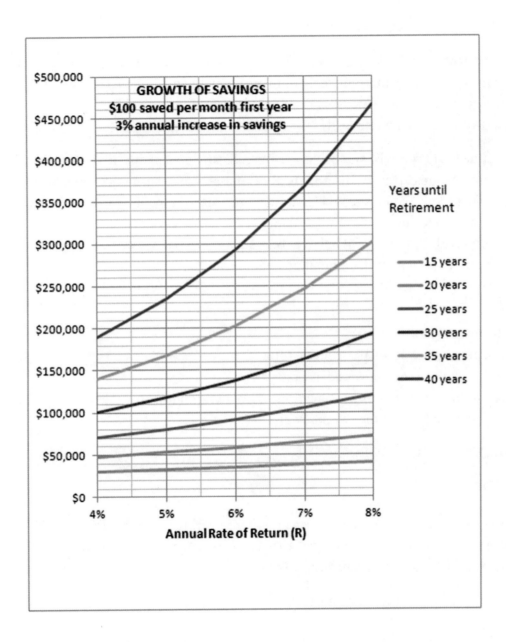

11.   ROI NEEDS WHEN RETIRED

A retirement account contains the assets you live on when retired. Presumably, no deposits are being made. You may make monthly or quarterly withdrawals that are transferred to a checking account for living expenses. The duration of retirement may be 20 to 40 years. The major question confronting retirees is "Will I outlive my assets?"

The answer depends upon the size of the account, the size of withdrawals, your budget for living expense, the rate of inflation, and the ROI of assets in the account. It will result that the ratio "withdrawal/account size" will determine the years in the future that the account will last. Years are measured from any date during retirement when you update the ratio. I show you the math involved so you will believe the results. The widely discussed 4% rule came from this math. I also discuss the limitations of the math.

Define the following symbols:

W = withdrawal ($) for first year
I = average annual rate of inflation during retirement
R = annual rate of return on invested assets
N = number of annual withdrawals supported, equals years from now that assets will last
PV = present value ($) of future withdrawals

Withdrawals grow with the inflation rate:

$$W_k = W(I+1)^{k-1}$$

W_k denotes the withdrawal on the kth year in retirement. K takes values from 1 to N. Withdrawals are made at the beginning of the year. For example, the withdrawal at the beginning of year #1 is W_1 and this equals W.

The present value of these N withdrawals is:

$$PV = \sum_{K=1}^{N} \frac{W(1+I)^{k-1}}{(1+R)^{k-1}}$$

PV is the amount of funds that are required at present to support the future N inflating withdrawals, assuming that funds remaining in the account grow at R per year. R is referred to as the discount rate for future withdrawals.[19]

This is rewritten as:

$$\frac{W}{PV} = \frac{1}{\sum_{K=1}^{N} \frac{(1+I)^{k-1}}{(1+R)^{k-1}}}$$

This is the formula for the ratio: "withdrawal/account size" and it shows the relation to all the variables we have defined. The account is depleted after the N withdrawals. The ratio W/PV is plotted below.

Dividends and interest payments are reinvested when paid. This reinvestment may be in a money market fund or in securities, depending upon your management. Your withdrawals will come from the cash-like assets, and if these cannot support your withdrawal needs, you will liquidate some securities. All will be liquidated at the end of N years.

Withdrawals are net of all guaranteed income sources. First, find your annual living expenses, including insurance and taxes paid. (A simple method is to find all annual debits from your checking account, including ATM withdrawals and fees.) From this figure subtract any pension benefits, social security benefits, and annuity benefits. The balance, if any, must come from withdrawals from your investment account.

---

[19] See the articles on PRESENT VALUE and DISCOUNTED CASH FLOW in Wikipedia (http://en.wikipedia.org/wiki/) and in http://sambaker.com/econ/irr/irr.html

Before we discuss the plots, let us talk about their limitations. First, we cannot know what the inflation rate will be N years into the future. The only remedy is to reevaluate this equation as times change. This equation tells you how long your assets will last from the current date. As one gets older, smaller values to the N variable may be selected.

Second, withdrawals include funds for income tax. Your tax rate may change as one ages. This formula does not model income tax rates.

Third, if living expenses increase on a permanent basis, such as needs for assisted living, look at the equation plots to assess how many years from that date your assets will last.

Fourth, one cannot know how long one will live. Choose a value of N that is larger than your expectations. Alternatively, set aside the current cost of, say, two years of assisted living in the retirement account. Compute the longevity of the remaining account size.

Finally, one cannot know what returns on investment your account will enjoy for the next 20 or more years. We can only look at past performance. Equity Index funds seek to track the total return of an index. They are not managed. We show the total returns of five index funds that cover different parts of the domestic and international stock market: the Schwab S&P 500 Fund (SWPPX), the Dow Jones Total Stock Market (SWTSX) as measured by the Wilshire 5000 Equity Index, the Schwab 1000 index of common stocks of US companies (SNXFX), the Schwab Small-Cap index (SWSSX) which tracks the second largest 1000 publicly traded US companies, and the Schwab International index (SWISX). These five indices encapsulate stock market performance. The following table exhibits the average annual returns (pre-tax) for these five funds. Data is as of June 30, 2013.[20]

---

[20] www.schwab.com/public/schwab/investing/accounts_products/. Look for Equity Index Funds. Values are pre-tax. Also refer to the Wall Street Journal. I am responsible for any errors in transcription.

	1 year	5 years	10 years	Since Inception[21]
SWPPX	20.45%	7.03%	7.25%	5.90%
SWTSX	21.41%	7.57%	8.07%	4.31%
SNXFX	20.71%	6.86%	7.40%	8.88%
SWSSX	26.24%	9.57%	9.41%	8.40%
SWISX	18.29%	-0.79%	7.47%	3.89%

The returns are geometric means and cover the periods ending at June 30, 2013. This means, for example, if you held SWPPX for five years ending June 30, 2013, your total return (dividends and capital gains are reinvested) would be the same as if you realized 7.03% return every year.

The first four funds cover US companies; the fifth covers foreign companies. The one year from June 30, 2012 to June 30, 2013 was unusual and we do not believe it illustrates what a portfolio could do over a retirement period. The longer durations yield more representative ROI values.

The lowest of the remaining fifteen numbers is -0.79%; the highest is 9.57%; the median is 7.4%; the third quartile is 8.4%; the first quartile is 5.9%. One may reasonably expect to

---

[21] Inception dates: SWPPX – 5/1997; SWTSX – 6/1999; SNXFX - 4/1991; SWSSX – 5/1997; SWISX – 5/1997

experience at least a 5.9% annual return on investment over a long period, but not more than 8.4%. The 50-50 value is 7.4%. [22]

Now turn to the plots of W/PV. Assume 2% annual inflation. Using a conservative 5.9% rate of return, the chart shows that your retirement assets will likely last 35 years from now if your first withdrawal is 5.0% of your beginning assets and subsequent withdrawals grow at 2% per year. [23] With 2.5% annual inflation your first withdrawal should be 4.7% of your beginning assets and subsequent annual withdrawals grow 2.5%..

Assets will last 30 years from now if you first withdraw 5.4% of your assets assuming 2% inflation, and 5.1% of your assets assuming 2.5% inflation. If you only expect to live 20 years from now, you may first withdraw 7.0% of your assets assuming 2% inflation, and 6.7% assuming 2.5% inflation. Recalculate these numbers as you grow older.

Reminder: The annual rate of return (R) in the charts is the growth from capital gains, dividends, and interest payments that accumulate in the account. It does not include deposits to the account. It is the time-weighted return of your account. TWR will determine investment performance while sidestepping deposits or withdrawals from the account.

The 5.9% value is the first quartile of fifteen values. Three quarters of the rates of return exceed this figure. This is an extremely conservative value. Pick whatever value you decide is reasonable. But do not shoot for the moon. These are rates of return expected to transpire on average over a twenty to forty year period.

---

[22] CalSTRS is the acronym commonly used for California State Teachers Retirement System. The following is a quote from page 76 of their CalSTRS Overview, Jan. 1, 2013. "The current investment return assumption for CalSTRS is 7.50 per cent. This is a common rate used by a number of large public plans."

[23] The last withdrawal occurs at the beginning of the 40th year.

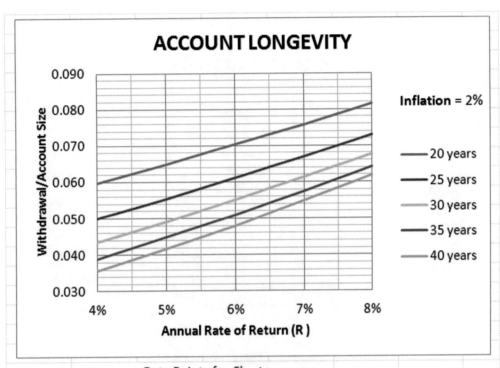

	Data Points for Chart				
	4%	**5%**	**7%**	**8%**	
20 years	0.0598	0.0649	0.0703	0.0759	0.0816
25 years	0.0500	0.0554	0.0611	0.0670	0.0731
30 years	0.0436	0.0492	0.0551	0.0613	0.0678
35 years	0.0390	0.0448	0.0510	0.0575	0.0642
40 years	0.0356	0.0416	0.0481	0.0548	0.0618

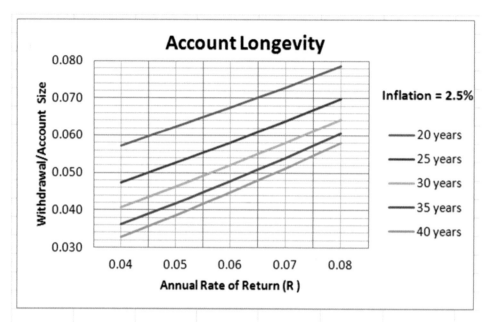

Data Points for the Chart					
	4%	5%	6%	7%	8%
20 years	0.0572	0.0623	0.0675	0.0729	0.0785
25 years	0.0474	0.0526	0.0581	0.0639	0.0698
30 years	0.0408	0.0463	0.0520	0.0581	0.0643
35 years	0.0362	0.0418	0.0478	0.0541	0.0607
40 years	0.0327	0.0385	0.0447	0.0512	0.0581

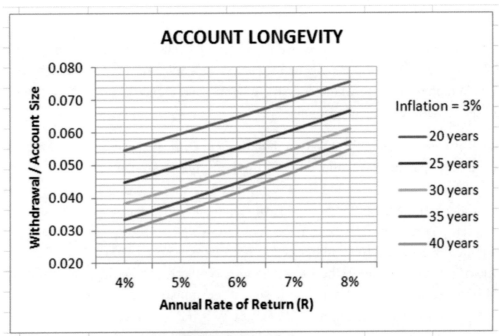

Data Points for the Chart					
	4%	5%	6%	7%	8%
20 years	0.0547	0.0597	0.0648	0.0701	0.0756
25 years	0.0448	0.0499	0.0553	0.0609	0.0667
30 years	0.0382	0.0434	0.0490	0.0549	0.0610
35 years	0.0335	0.0389	0.0446	0.0508	0.0572
40 years	0.0300	0.0355	0.0414	0.0478	0.0545

It is emphasized: The first withdrawal is W and occurs at the beginning of the first year. It allows increases in your annual withdrawals in line with the inflation rate.

Suppose your assets include owned real estate, such as your home. Use these assets as a safety factor to be liquidated when your securities account is depleted.

The performance of your investment account in retirement should be measured against these rates of return values. Account management must yield a 5.9% rate of return, or better. The question is: Which of the several methods of ROR measurement discussed in this booklet can be used to assess retirement accounts?

In Chapter 9 we advise using the TWR methodology to evaluate account rate of return. It must exceed 5.9% per year. Account dollar growth may be less---the account may indeed decline. This is normal behavior but the TWR value determines account longevity. To demonstrate the evolution and longevity of your account, construct the spreadsheet illustrated on the next page. The example shown is of a 30 year retirement budget based upon 2% annual inflation, $100,000 beginning retirement account value, and a 5.0 percent annual rate of return. To achieve the 30 year longevity, the first benefit payment must be $4919. (4.9% of assets) The following table shows the annual benefits and the evolving ending balance in the account. The account longevity is indeed thirty years.

Input data includes the blue cells (required) and Exceptional Expenses (optional). Examples of exceptional expenses are home remodel, major vacation trip, new automobile, medical surgery, etc. Enter their costs and years planned, and see the impact on retirement account longevity. Email me and I will send you the Excel file for your use. Instructions included.

Verification of Retirement Account Longevity			
Initial Account Balance:			$100,000.00
Investment Annual Return:			5.00%
Annual Inflation of Basic Expenses:			2.00%
Initial Annual Benefit:			$4,919.00
Date of first Benefit Payment:			6/1/2013
Dates	Basic Benefits	Prior Year Exceptional Expenses	Account Balance
6/1/2013	$4,919.00	$0.00	$95,081.00
6/1/2014	$5,017.38	$0.00	$94,817.67
6/1/2015	$5,117.73		$94,440.83
5/31/2016	$5,220.08		$93,942.79
6/1/2017	$5,324.48		$93,315.44
6/1/2018	$5,430.97		$92,550.24
6/1/2019	$5,539.59		$91,638.16
5/31/2020	$5,650.38		$90,569.68
6/1/2021	$5,763.39		$89,334.77
6/1/2022	$5,878.66		$87,922.85
6/1/2023	$5,996.23		$86,322.76

5/31/2024	$6,116.16		$84,522.74
6/1/2025	$6,238.48		$82,510.40
6/1/2026	$6,363.25		$80,272.66
6/1/2027	$6,490.52		$77,795.78
5/31/2028	$6,620.33		$75,065.24
6/1/2029	$6,752.73		$72,065.77
6/1/2030	$6,887.79		$68,781.27
6/1/2031	$7,025.54		$65,194.79
5/31/2032	$7,166.05		$61,288.48
6/1/2033	$7,309.38		$57,043.53
6/1/2034	$7,455.56		$52,440.14
6/1/2035	$7,604.67		$47,457.48
5/31/2036	$7,756.77		$42,073.58
6/1/2037	$7,911.90		$36,265.36
6/1/2038	$8,070.14		$30,008.49
6/1/2039	$8,231.54		$23,277.37
5/31/2040	$8,396.17		$16,045.06
6/1/2041	$8,564.10		$8,283.22
6/1/2042	$8,735.38		-$38.00
6/1/2043	$8,910.09		-$8,949.99

12. THE BOTTOM LINE

 Internal Rate of Return (IRR) is the growth of your account as modified by all cash flows. If you deposited funds (and purchased stock) at a market low and sold the stock and withdrew the funds at a market high, the IRR measure will detect this. Time-Weighted Return (TWR) will not detect these cash flows. Whereas IRR accounts for all cash flows, TWR excludes them. TWR measures only percentage market gains or losses of invested funds. It thus evaluates the management of your account.

The basic Dietz equation computes a return comparable to IRR values. View it as a quick approximate evaluator and only for one-quarter periods. Obtain an annual return by compounding four quarterly returns.

Use TWR to compare your account with stock funds that show their returns as the growth of $10,000 over a time period. We provide a spreadsheet that facilitates this calculation. Use the TWR method to find your SEC Total Return when comparing your account management to stock fund management. Incorporate all fees identified by the SEC.

Retirement accounts have an annual rate of return used in their planning. The TWR method computes this rate of return. Use it to assess your account management. ***Do not confuse percent account growth with TWR values.*** Savings account growth may appear reasonable, but hide a subpar TWR indicating poor management. The TWR value determines whether you can reach your goal of a certain account size at the retirement date.

When living off an account during retirement, account value may increase or decrease at a low rate, even in the presence of satisfactory TWR. This should not worry you because the ***TWR value determines account longevity.*** We provide a spreadsheet to show the evolution of account value and demonstrate its longevity.

GLOSSARY

Algebraic Symbols:

The asterisk * is used in Excel spreadsheets to signify "multiplication". It replaces ×.

The Greek capital letter pi $\prod$ signifies multiplication. It is used in chapter 4. The expression $\prod_{k=1}^{N} term\ k$ signifies the product of N different terms.

The Greek capital letter sigma $\sum$ signifies addition. It is used in chapter 11. The expression $\sum_{k=1}^{N} term\ k$ signifies the sum of N different terms.

Acronyms

The reader will obtain more detailed explanations by searching for the terms on the Internet, using Google, Bing or other search engines. Also, look into Wikipedia.

ETF signifies an Exchange Traded Fund.

SEC signifies the Securities and Exchange Commission. It is the government body that regulates securities sales and promotion, among other things.

FINRA signifies Financial Industry Regulatory Agency, Inc. It is a private organization whose chief role is to protect investors by maintaining the fairness of the US capital markets.

"Multiplier" defined in this book is "1+ROI". An account has a specific ROI and multiplier value over any time period that contains no cash flows. A value, say $1000, invested in the account at the beginning of the period, will have the value "multiplier×$1000" at the end of the period. Multipliers are used throughout TWR and IRR equations.

ABOUT THIS BOOK

The author has an MS degree in mathematics from the University of Washington. He was an aerospace engineer for 38 years, taught algebra at Santa Barbara City College for eleven years and then retired. To fill his time subsequently, he began to manage his retirement account---depositing and withdrawing funds, identifying stocks to purchase and sell. To grade his management he researched methods to calculate rates of return and discovered a hidden story behind the methods. This booklet tells this story as an algebra teacher would teach it.

The simple formula for Return on Investment during a period---the one you probably know by heart---does not compute in the presence of cash flows (deposits or withdrawals) during the period. The modification, published by Joseph Dietz in 1966, incorporates cash flows, but the approach is not exact. The more recent Time Weighted Return method circumvents cash flows exactly. Finally, the Internal Rate of Return method includes all cash flows and their dates. All methods can give different values and they do have different meanings.

This book explains the equations behind all methods mentioned and instructs on the construction of a personal spreadsheet. Alternately, Excel spreadsheets may be obtained from the author's email address. Finally, the reader's stock broker may have the methods installed on company computers, and will provide help in accessing and using them. For all alternatives, this book provides insight into each method and its interpretation.

Printed in the United States
By Bookmasters